TALKING

Prayers for C
World'

Selected & Illustrated by

TO GOD

...dren from the
...Religions

Demi

Wisdom Tales

Wisdom Tales is an imprint of World Wisdom, Inc.

Library of Congress Cataloging-in-Publication Data

Names: Demi, author.
Title: Talking to God : prayers for children from the world's religions /
selected and illustrated by Demi.
Description: Bloomington, IN : Wisdom Tales, 2017. |
Identifiers: LCCN 2017005578 (print) | LCCN 2017017113 (ebook) | ISBN
9781937786700 (epub) | ISBN 9781937786694 (casebound : alk. paper)
Subjects: LCSH: Children--Prayers and devotions.
Classification: LCC BL625.5 (ebook) | LCC BL625.5 .D46 2017 (print) | DDC
204/.33--dc23
LC record available at https://lccn.loc.gov/2017005578

Printed in China on acid-free paper.

Production Date: April 2017
Plant & Location: Printed through Asia Pacific Offset Limited
Job/Batch#: Q17040197

For information address Wisdom Tales,
P.O. Box 2682, Bloomington, Indiana 47402-2682
www.wisdomtalespress.com

Author's Preface

What more precious gift could a child receive from its parents than the timeless wisdom contained in the world's religions? For each of these heavenly-ordained traditions has important lessons to instruct our children and help mold their characters.

In this book of short prayers from across the world's religions,[1] children can learn the great value of conversing or talking to God. Here they will find time-honored prayers of praise, prayers of petition, prayers of gratitude, and prayers of blessing. They will learn that through the grace of prayer we enter into a heavenly relationship with the Divine, the fruits of that relationship being the virtues of humility and charity: that is, to submit ourselves to almighty God above us and to love our neighbor beside us.

Through my accompanying illustrations I hope to bring each passage of prayer to life before the reader's eyes. Moving from St. Mark's Cathedral in Venice to King Solomon's Temple and the Dome of the Rock in Jerusalem to the River Ganges in India; from North America to Central Africa to China and Japan—each new illustration transports the reader to their sacred destination, where they can experience the religion directly at its source.

Thus, in combining text and illustrations, *Talking to God* aims to introduce young readers to the Truth, Prayer, and Virtue—the lived spirituality—of the world's religions. It aims to show them how to forge a loving relationship with their Creator and Lord, and how to foster tolerance and respect for their fellow believers in the sacred religions of the world.

—DEMI

1 My categorization of religions follows Huston Smith's bestselling work, *The World's Religions*, with some minor modifications. I have chosen to begin my book with Christianity (rather than Hinduism) because it is the most familiar tradition for western readers. I have also included a section on Japanese Shintoism rather than Confucianism, given that the Chinese tradition is already represented by Taoism. For further details on the various prayers selected and the illustrations presented, please see the Appendix.

Christianity

Our Father in heaven,
Holy is Your name.
Your kingdom come.
Your will be done
On earth as it is in heaven.
Give us this day our daily bread.
And forgive us our debts,
As we forgive our debtors.
And do not lead us into temptation,
But deliver us from the evil one.
For Yours is the kingdom and the
power and the glory forever. Amen.
(The Lord's Prayer)

The Lord is my shepherd;
I shall not want.
He makes me to lie down in green pastures;
He leads me beside the still waters.
He restores my soul;
He leads me in the paths of righteousness for His name's sake.
Yea, though I walk through the valley of the shadow of death,
I will fear no evil;
For You are with me.
(Psalm 23:1–4)

Hail Mary, full of grace,
The Lord is with you;
Blessed are you among women,
And blessed is the fruit of your
    womb, Jesus.
Holy Mary, Mother of God,
Pray for us sinners,
Now and at the hour of our
    death. Amen.
(*Ave Maria*)

Lord, make me an instrument of Your peace;
Where there is hatred, let me sow love; Where there is injury, pardon;
Where there is error, truth; Where there is doubt, faith;
Where there is despair, hope; Where there is darkness, light;
And where there is sadness, joy.
O Divine Master, grant that I may not so much seek
To be consoled as to console;
To be understood as to understand;
To be loved as to love.
For it is in giving that we receive;
It is in pardoning that we are pardoned;
And it is in dying that we are born to eternal life.
(Francis of Assisi)

Thank you for the world so sweet,
Thank you for the food we eat,
Thank you for the birds that sing,
Thank you God for everything.
(Mealtime Blessing)

I am little;
My heart is pure;
May none dwell therein,
Save Jesus alone.
(Protestant Prayer)

Judaism

Hear, O Israel: the Lord our God is one Lord. You shall love the Lord your God with all your heart, with all your soul, and with all your strength.
(*Shema*)

The Lord bless you and keep you;
The Lord make his face shine upon
   you,
And be gracious to you.
The Lord lift up His countenance
   upon you,
And give you peace.
(Numbers 6:24–26)

Wherever I go, only You (Lord)!
Wherever I stand, only You!
Just You! Again You! Always You!
You! You! You!
When things are good, You!
When things are bad, You!
You! You! Always You!
(Nachman of Bratslav)

Blessed are You, Lord our God,
King of the universe,
Who has sanctified us with His
  commandments,
And commanded us to kindle the
  lights of the holy Sabbath.
(*Shabbat* Prayer)

Islam

God is most great. God is most great.
I testify that there is no god but God.
I testify that Muhammad is the
   Prophet of God.
Come to prayer; come to salvation.
God is most great. God is most great.
There is no god but God.
(The Call to Prayer)

God is sufficient for us.
He is the best protector.
(Koran 3:173)

In the Name of God, the
  Clement, the Merciful.
Praise be to God, the Lord of
  the worlds.
The Clement, the Merciful.
Master of the Day of
  Judgment.
You we worship and from You
  we seek help.
Lead us on the straight path.
The path of those You have
  blessed,
Not of those who incur Your
  anger,
Nor of those who go astray.
(Koran 1:1–7)

To God we belong and to
Him we shall return.
(Koran 2:156)

Hinduism

🕉

O God, you are the giver of life;
You are the remover of pain and
    sorrow;
You are the bestower of happiness.
May your light destroy our sins.
May you illumine our mind.
And may You lead us along the
    righteous path.
(*Gayatri Mantra*)

May the Lord protect us.
May the Lord nourish us.
May the Lord strengthen us.
May we realize the Lord.
May we live with love for all;
May we live in peace with all.
(*Katha Upanishad*)

Buddhism

May all beings be well and secure;
May all beings be happy!
(*Metta Sutta*)

I take refuge in the Buddha.
I take refuge in the Law of the
   Buddha.
I take refuge in the Community of
   the Buddha.
(The Triple Refuge)

Taoism

In dealing with others,
Know how to be gentle and kind.
(Lao Tzu)

Shintoism

O spirits, wash away my sins from me.
(Traditional Prayer)

American Plains Indian

O Great Spirit,
Whose voice I hear in the winds,
And whose breath gives life to all the
    world, hear me!
I am small and weak.
I need your strength and wisdom.
(Chief Yellow Lark, Lakota)

Central African

I shall sing a song of praise to God.
Strike the chords upon the drum.
God, who gives us all good things—
Strike the chords upon the drum.
Friends, and wealth, and wisdom—
Strike the chords upon the drum.
(Luba Song)

O Praise the Lord, all you nations;
Praise Him, all you peoples.

For His merciful kindness is great toward us;
And the truth of the Lord endures forever.
Praise the Lord! (Psalm 117:1–2)

Notes on the Prayers

Christianity

8: The words of the Lord's Prayer derive from the Sermon on the Mount (Matthew 6:9–13, Luke 11:1–4), where Jesus instructs his disciples: "This, then, is how you should pray, Our Father . . ."

9: "The Lord is my shepherd" is without doubt the most beloved of all the psalms in the Bible. It is traditionally ascribed to David, the prophet-king of Israel.

10: The "Hail Mary" (*Ave Maria* in Latin) is a popular Christian prayer based on the first two words of the Angel Gabriel to the Virgin Mary (Luke 1:28) during the Annunciation.

11: The "Peace Prayer" is an anonymous prayer often attributed to St. Francis of Assisi (c. 1181–1226) because it embodies his spirit of simplicity and poverty.

12: This simple mealtime blessing was composed by the poet Edith Rutter Leatham and was first published in 1908.

13: This is a traditional Volga German bedtime prayer from Russia.

Judaism

14: The *Shema Yisrael* ("Hear O Israel") is the central prayer in the Jewish prayer book (*Siddur*). It is often the first portion of Scripture (see Deuteronomy 6:4–9) that a Jewish child learns to recite.

15: The "priestly blessing" (Numbers 6:24–26) was traditionally recited each morning by the Jewish Levites as a benediction upon the Israelites after the sacrifice in the Temple in Jerusalem.

16: Rabbi Nachman of Bratslav (1772–1810) was the great-grandson of the renowned Baal Shem Tov (c. 1700–1760), founder of the mystical Hasidic movement in Europe. Rabbi Nachman's teachings on prayer emphasized closeness to God and speaking to Him "as you would with a best friend."

17: This prayer is recited on Friday evenings by the mother of the house after the lighting of the candles at the Sabbath (*Shabbat*) meal.

Islam

18: The Muslim *adhan*, or "call to prayer," is recited by the muezzin five times a day: at dawn, midday, mid-afternoon, sunset, and nightfall, when Muslims perform their five daily prayers.

19: This is one of the most popular Koranic prayers recited by Muslims, especially in cases of danger.

20: The *Fatihah*, or "opening" chapter of the Koran, is recited by Muslims during each of their five daily prayers.

21: This Koranic prayer is often recited as a benediction when a Muslim passes away.

Hinduism

22: The *Gayatri mantra* is a famous prayer to Gayatri, the Hindu *shakti*, or goddess, who manifests herself through the sun.

23: This is the opening prayer to the ancient *Katha Upanishad*, which forms part of the *sruti*, or revealed scriptures, in Hinduism.

Buddhism

24: This prayer of benediction from the *Metta Sutta*, or "Scripture of Loving-kindness," teaches showing love and compassion (*metta*) for all creatures, both living and non-living.

25: Monks and nuns, as well as lay people, recite the prayer of the Triple Refuge when taking ordination vows to become Buddhists. They pledge to be faithful to: (1) the Buddha Gautama, (2) the teaching (*dharma*) of the Buddha, and (3) the community (*sangha*) of the Buddha.

Taoism & Shintoism

26: Lao Tzu, the founder of Taoism, presents this teaching on the treatment of others in the eighth chapter of the *Tao Te Ching*, or "Book on the Way and Its Virtue."

27: This popular prayer of purification in Shintoism, the Japanese "way of the gods," is often performed at a waterfall.

American Plains Indian & Central African

28: This Native American prayer is attributed to the Lakota medicine man Chief Yellow Lark and is said to have been composed in 1887.

29: This traditional praise song is from the Luba people of the Democratic Republic of the Congo in Central Africa.

General

30-31: This psalm has a universal meaning that speaks to the very heart of all religions: showing praise and gratitude to the Divine.

Notes on the Illustrations

Christianity

8: Children praying inside a church. Above, Christ is seated in glory surrounded by angels and symbols of the four Evangelists; below, the Virgin and Child are accompanied by the saints in Heaven.

9: Christ depicted with arms outstretched to welcome all to the "good news" of the Gospel.

10: A church service with a priest carrying the cross aloft and a deacon swinging a censer containing incense. Above are figures of angels and saints proclaiming the words of scripture.

11: St. Francis of Assisi preaching a famous sermon to the birds, enjoining them to praise God for the many gifts they have received from Him.

12: St. Mark's Cathedral in Venice, Italy, with nuns feeding and playing with the pigeons.

13: Children gather colorful Easter eggs in front of a church, based on the Unitarian Church in Milton, Massachusetts. A child holds a banner aloft depicting Christ carrying the Bible and a staff, surrounded by symbols of the four Evangelists.

Judaism

14: A rabbi in a Jewish synagogue reads to the faithful from the scrolls of the Torah.

15: Jews praying and reciting scripture at the Western Wall in Jerusalem, the last surviving wall from the ancient Temple Mount built at the time of Herod the Great.

16: Jews pass by an Eastern European synagogue decorated with the symbol of the Star of David.

17: A Jewish family celebrating the sacred *Shabbat* meal at sunset on Friday evening.

Islam

18: An *imam*, or religious leader, presents the Friday sermon to the faithful from the *minbar*, or pulpit, inside a mosque.

19: The Dome of the Rock, on the Temple Mount in Jerusalem, from where the Prophet Muhammad is said to have made his "night journey" (*miraj*) to Heaven.

20: The Delhi Mosque in India, built by the Mughal emperor Shah Jahan, who also constructed the famous Taj Mahal in Agra, India. The large courtyard of the Delhi Mosque can hold as many as 25,000 believers.

21: Sufi whirling dervishes seek union with the Divine through ecstatic music, song, and dance.

Hinduism

22: A Hindu temple, based on the South Indian temples of Madurai, depicting the many gods and goddesses in statuary form. Women dressed in saris stand at the entrance to the temple.

23: Pilgrims bathing and purifying themselves in the sacred Ganges River in Benares, India.

Buddhism

24: Buddhist monks sit in meditation before the Buddha Siddartha Gautama.

25: Buddhist monks and children pray at a Buddhist temple, based on the Rey Tsang Temple in Redmond, Washington.

Taoism & Shintoism

26: A Taoist monk prostrates in prayer.

27: Priests and laypeople pray at a Shinto shrine in Japan. Processions and music are common during such festivals.

American Plains Indian & Central African

28: The American Plains Indians solemnly offer their prayers to *Wakan Tanka*, the Great Spirit, through the ritual smoke of the sacred pipe.

29: The Luba tribe of the Democratic Republic of the Congo use music and dance to sing God's praises.

General

30-31: The faithful from the world's religions are all alike in praising and giving thanks to the Divine.